PA
PRINCIPLE

By Antoine Delers

In collaboration with
Isabelle Van Steenkiste

Translation by Carly Probert

Management & Marketing 50MINUTES.com

PARETO'S PRINCIPLE

KEY POINTS

- **Names:** Pareto's principle, Pareto's rule, Pareto's law, the 80/20 rule, the law of the vital few
- **Uses:**
  - Economics: Business management (quality management, customer management, production management, stock control, human resources, etc.), creating commercial and marketing strategies, etc.
  - Physics, sociology and statistics
  - Private sector: time management, task organization, etc.
- **Why is it successful?** According to Pareto's principle, '80% of effects are the product of 20% of causes'. This ratio allows you to quickly identify the essential part of any activity. The model is found in many areas of daily life and in the business world. For example, when a business wants to identify the customers that generate the most revenue. If the 80/20 ratio is considered, the company can focus on the 20% of customers that generate 80% of its turnover to try and make them loyal customers.
- **Keywords:** Vilfredo Pareto, Pareto's principle, the 80/20 rule, ABC analysis, turnover, Joseph Juran, time management, customer relations, relationship marketing, CRM, Pareto chart, Long Tail theory, Pareto efficiency

INTRODUCTION

History

Pareto's principle is an analysis and decision-making tool created by Vilfredo Pareto (1848-1923) at the end of the 19th century in 1897. The Italian economist and sociologist, who studied at the Polytechnic University of Turin in Italy, is considered to be the founding father of what is now called 'Pareto's Principle'. By studying the wealth of his country he found that only 20% of people owned 80% of the total wealth. He then applied this law to other states such as Russia, France and Switzerland and found the same results.

However, it wasn't until the 1940s that Joseph Juran (1904-2008), an American engineer working in quality management, recognized the 80/20 theory and named it after Vilfredo Pareto.

Definition of the model

Pareto's principle comes from the observation that 20% of causes are responsible for 80% of the effects. In other words, in the world of business, 20% of customers are responsible for 80% of turnover. By identifying this 20% (the most important customers) companies can pay more attention to them to save time and money. According to Joseph Juran, Pareto's principle can be applied universally in the corporate domain and can be found in all sectors of society. You can even use the principle in most areas of daily life. However, we will see that, both in business and other areas, the 80/20 ratio is not always respected but does give an idea of reality.

THEORY – THE CONCEPT

INITIAL CONTEXT

In the forties, Joseph Juran observed that a minority of faults caused the majority of problems in the production line. Quickly recognizing the 80/20 ratio (80% of problems are caused by 20% of faults), he attributed this theory to Vilfredo Pareto in the early twentieth century. Joseph Juran, during his research on quality management, showed that causes can be separated into two groups: those which are vital (in this case, 20% of faults) and those which are secondary, representing the remaining 80%. By isolating the most problematic faults (those that cause 80% of problems) Joseph Juran could focus on these further and significantly reduce the problems in the production line.

EXTRA INFORMATION

Joseph Juran's principle was originally called 'the vital few and trivial many'. Despite the considerable contribution of the economist, the 'Pareto's principle' name is still remembered more, probably because it sounds better than the name given by Joseph Juran.

APPLICATIONS IN BUSINESS

Today, Pareto's principle has many applications in business and in areas of personal management and research efficiency. Applications in business are mainly used for customer management and human resources. For example, 20% of employees produce 80% of the work. But it is also used in business strategies, knowing that 20% of products generate 80% of profits. In this book we will discuss in depth the application of this principle to the corporate sector. The following points present the many different uses in a clear and succinct way to help you understand Pareto's principle.

Pareto's principle as a tool in relationship marketing

As we have already mentioned, one of the most important applications of Pareto's principle is the customer management of a company. Many studies show that 20% of customers are responsible for 80% of sales. These customers are the most important to the company. It is therefore better to make them loyal customers in order to ensure maximum retention, particularly through relationship marketing.

USEFUL INFORMATION

Relationship marketing is a tool that lets you create and maintain a relationship between a brand and its customers by awarding gifts or discounts, or through invitations or advice. The goal is to develop a long term relationship with customers, as retention costs are lower compared to the costs of attracting new customers.

Another application of Pareto's principle is managing customer relations: 20% of customers are the source of 80% of complaints. If the 20% of customers used in the above example are the same as this 20%, the company will have no difficulty meeting their demands since it is already focusing on retention. Unfortunately, this is hardly ever the case: the 20% of important customers are rarely the same as the 20% responsible for 80% of complaints. In this case, it is more difficult for the company to clearly identify each customer category and assign them most of the attention. The company must then decide on its priority and choose between revenue and complaints management (generating customer satisfaction).

Pareto's principle as a quality control tool

A second application, used by Joseph Juran, is that of control and quality management in a production line. If 20% of faults cause 80% of the problems, the company can concentrate its efforts on addressing the faults in question in order to improve quality. Other similar applications are also valid:

- 20% of machine set-up time can solve 80% of problems;
- 20% of the production line is responsible for 80% of the final product.

Other uses of Pareto's principle

- Personal management tool: 20% of the work produces 80% of the results.
- Risk management tool: 20% of the risks cause 80% of the consequences.
- Logistics management tool: 20% of products generate 80% of storage costs.
- Stock management tool: 20% of the total number of products represents 80% of the total value of the stock.
- Sales management tool: 20% of products generate 80% of profits, etc.

WHAT IF THE RULE WAS USED REGULARLY?

What if Pareto's principle was always used in business today? Should we get as close to the 80/20 ratio as possible to survive?

Take the example already studied: A company, after studying its customers, finds that only 10% of its customers contribute to 90% of its turnover. This situation is quite worrying as its capital of key customers is low. If the company were to lose just a few of them, its revenue would fall drastically. In this case, moving away from the standard 80/20 could be fatal for the company. There are two possible solutions:

- Should the company decide to look after its major customers to retain them? But this simplistic solution does not solve its problems because their future relies completely on these customers;
- Or, done alongside the first option, should the company choose to make the other customers loyal to return to a better balance. At this point, it is interesting to think about how to get customers to become loyal, in order to return to an average ratio that's more secure.

The second example shows that moving away from the norm is not necessarily harmful to the company. Imagine that same company which, after its customer study, notes that it has no main customers and 30% of its most important buyers generate 70% of its turnover. Although close to the 80/20 rule (but still not reaching Pareto's equilibrium) the company is in less trouble than in the previous scenario. Of course, the activity is probably dispersed, but the loss of some customers would not affect the situation as much as the 90/10 ratio and is not a cause for concern. This could be problematic in terms of cost per customer: the costs of managing customer communications are actually more important. In this case, returning to the 80/20 balance would lead to future success.

Adapting Pareto's principle to reach the 80/20 ratio is not a goal in itself. It all depends on the activity of the company and its sector. A supermarket company is likely to have many small customers, as is normal for the sector, while an aircraft manufacturer has fewer customers, but they are inevitably bigger. Therefore, the sector influences the ratio of Pareto's principle, and it shouldn't always be 80/20.

ADVANTAGES OF PARETO'S PRINCIPLE

The benefits of using Pareto's principle are infinite. Most of them have already been mentioned in previous chapters. A company that knows its Pareto ratio for each department can improve its effectiveness, including:

- Better managing its risks. By knowing the most important risks and those that are easy to correct, a company can concentrate on its core business;
- Knowing its customers better. A company can set its communication strategy and target the most important consumers. It's important to know the characteristics of 20% of the largest customers, including their source, their type of industry (in the case of professionals) or their age and gender (in the case of individuals). By doing this, it can create new prospects that match the characteristics. The target consumers are similar to the best customers; the company has a better chance of bringing them from the prospective stage to the consumer stage;
- Limiting costs. In a production line, knowing which points consume the most energy but provide lower efficiency can enable the company to adapt, remove or modify the most expensive elements;
- Limiting time loss. By knowing which activities are the most productive, a manager can focus on them to improve their performance.

LIMITS AND EXTENSIONS OF THE MODEL

LIMITS AND CRITICISMS OF THE MODEL

Pareto's principle, despite its universal character, is not always true in every sector and every department. We looked at an example of a limit with supermarkets, an area where it is unlikely that 20% of customers bring 80% of sales. The model must be adapted to the sector and the corporate department. We can highlight two criticisms: first, the 80/20 ratio is not always observed in reality. Secondly, focusing on the 20% is not always the best solution.

An inexact model

The first criticism of the principle points out that it's not scientifically accurate. Getting an 80/20 ratio for each department of a company is actually impossible. However, the original idea of the model is not contradicted. In Joseph Juran's theory, the effects should be separated into two groups. The first group includes the effects that are few, but have important consequences. The second group includes the effects that are numerous, but have limited consequences. If these groups do not correspond exactly to 20% and 80%, ratios of 10/90 or 5/95 can be used and are even expected in some situations.

An ineffecient model

The second criticism concerns the relative efficiency of Pareto's principle. If 80% of the company's products are not often sold, they can still represent a considerable margin of sales (say 20%). If storage costs for these products are low, the company can afford to continue selling them, even if they attract fewer customers. We will see in the next point that Pareto's principle is linked to another important principle called the Long Tail theory.

EXTENSIONS AND RELATED MODELS

The ABC model

The ABC model is an improvement on Pareto's principle. The new model argues that, with Pareto's principle, intermediate categories are ignored and it is difficult to judge their importance. By classifying the effects into three categories (A, B and C), a company does not neglect the effects that are less important than the 20% and acknowledges their importance in terms of consequences. The three classes can be divided like this:

- Class A: 20% of customers who bring 80% of sales;
- Class B: 30% of customers who bring 15% of sales;
- Class C: 50% of customers who bring 5% of sales.

Class B is risky, as investing time and money there can have different effects. Since these factors were neglected by Pareto, the ABC model is more accurate and takes into account the intermediate categories.

The Long Tail theory

The Long Tail theory is related to Pareto's principle and complements it. This model distributes the revenue of a company to all of its products, including specific assets – which represent an important part of turnover – which are characterized by:

- Low sales of specific products;
- A high number of special products (often more than 80% of the total number of products).

In the case of a bookseller, for example, the specific products relate to the published works that only sell a few copies per year. Given the costs and the space needed for stock, it is impossible for a bookseller to only offer those books. It must focus on books that sell well, such as bestsellers, to balance the scales.

The link with Pareto's principle is the fact that, here, only a minority of items represent the majority of sales. A traditional business must focus on these products. However, e-commerce sites are an exception.

EXTRA INFORMATION

E-commerce, also known as online sales, limits the product storage costs, since they didn't have to be presented in shops, just simply stocked in a ware-house. The e-merchants can therefore offer a greater range of products for sale. E-commerce also allows the company to extend its catchment area at lower costs.

When following Pareto's principle, we shouldn't focus only on the most important 20%. The Long Tail theory in e-commerce enables the consideration of the remaining 80% since the additional cost is minimal and the yield is high. Amazon is a perfect example of the Long Tail theory. As an e-commerce site, the company can offer an impressive number of publications that were previously hard to find in stores. Although this case benefits from the data available on the internet, it is still an obvious example of the limits of Pareto's principle. As you can see, it can be beneficial for some companies to focus on more than the 20% of products that sell more.

APPLICATIONS OF PARETO'S PRINCIPLE

In this chapter, we can apply what we have learned so far. We will start by creating a Pareto chart, which is useful to visually identify the most important 20%. The example is about a vendor and its customers and it is intentionally simplistic to make it easy to understand. A more comprehensive case study can be found at the end of this chapter.

FORMATTING THE TABLE

The first step is to prepare a table. As we want to find the most important 20%, it is advisable to sort the data in descending order to immediately detect the important elements.

In the first column, write a list of factors to observe (for example, a customer list). In the second column, there must be variables that correspond to the factors (for example, the amount of purchases made by individual customers).

Then we need to calculate the percentage of each object (in this case, each customer) and the cumulative percentage. This percentage will draw a line of cumulative percentages in Pareto's chart. By adding all the data, the 80% threshold will emerge.

EXTRA INFORMATION

It is not always easy to identify the customers because there are so many individuals in the retail sector. Companies can still develop ways to acquire a database of reliable customers; using a loyalty card is a prime example.

Once you've broken down the information, you should get a table like this:

Customer	Purchases	Percentage (%)	Cumulative percentage
A	9700	24,84	24,84
B	8200	21,00	45,84
C	6900	17,67	63,51
D	4970	12,73	76,24
E	1890	4,84	81,08
F	1660	4,25	85,33
G	1540	3,94	89,27
H	1230	3,15	92,42
I	800	2,05	94,47
J	610	1,56	96,03
K	520	1,33	97,36
L	380	0,97	98,34
M	350	0,90	99,23
N	200	0,51	99,74
O	100	0,26	100,00
Total	39050	100,00	

This example includes a total of 15 customers, identified by letters A-O and sorted in descending order according to the amount of purchases made (the data in the second column). It can, for example, be the results of a home seller and its customer portfolio. The third column corresponds to the percentage of purchases of each customer, based on the total amount. The fourth column calculates the cumulative percentage (the addition of all percentages). All customers add up to 100% of the sales.

The data in red corresponds to the 80% of customers researched in Pareto's principle. As expected, we have approximately 27% of customers (4 out of 15) which generate approximately 76% of sales. The vendor will focus its attention on this 27% of customers.

Notice that it's possible to apply the ABC rule in this case, since there is a profitable intermediate category for the seller. The customers concerned (E, F, G, H, I and J) represent 40% of consumers and generate 20% of sales: they are identified in blue.

CREATING THE GRAPH

We must now draw the graph (for example, using Excel). The graph is usually paired with a line graph of a value curve which represents the last column of the table. This approach is optional: it is possible to discuss the results from the simple table.

Here is the graph created from the data:

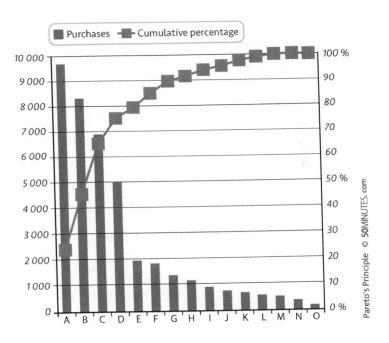

The x-axis shows the customers and the y-axis corresponds to the amount of sales. The red bars represent the total amount purchased by all of the customers in the vendor's portfolio, while the blue line represents the cumulative percentage of sales (the data shown as a percentage on the right). We will interpret these results in the following sections of this chapter.

IDENTIFYING THE MOST IMPORTANT 20%

For step three, we will interpret the graph (and/or table) to identify the most important 20%. In the case of the customers, we can easily identify the total sales generated from a particular customer. The result does not necessarily correspond to the 80/20 rule, but it is important to know the factors that affect each of the studied areas.

Initial observations

- Approximately 20% of customers (A, B, C and D) generate 76% of turnover (a ratio close to Pareto's 80/20).
- Most of the seller's attention should be devoted to making these important customers loyal.

- The ABC method does not neglect the intermediate factors which, in this case, constitute almost 20% of turnover.

TAKING ACTION

Courses of action

The final step involves taking action based on the results to improve the yield from corporate strategies. Actions can be diverse:
- Correcting problems in a factory;
- Rewarding highly productive employees;
- Identifying prospects;
- Making customers loyal, etc.

Customer retention can be done via advertising, customized promotions or other retention strategies. For example, a company could invite customers to a trade fair.

To complete this example, we can imagine that our home seller, who identified four customers and implemented a loyalty strategy, decided to seek new prospects to increase its turnover. To achieve this new goal, he can use a particular tool called 'RFM segmentation'.

Recommendations
- It's pointless using Pareto's principle if you don't want to take action.
- The method is not accurate, as some sectors shouldn't necessarily have an 80/20 ratio.
- Pareto's principle cannot be used in all sectors.
- This method does not consider intermediate categories.
- As we have seen with the Long Tail theory in e-commerce, the less frequent values can be beneficial in some cases.

CASE STUDY – A PRODUCTION LINE

Introduction to the problem

Our case study concerns an industry and its production line. In this company, the production line is experiencing recurrent interruptions throughout the year. Together they add up to a total of 1033 hours, which is just over a month of inactivity. To make up for the loss of working hours, the manager, who noticed that the dynamic was not logical, identifies the ten common causes of line stoppage. He then estimates an average stoppage time (in hours) and provides a count of occurrences for each cause. Using Pareto's principle, he hopes to identify the main factors that disrupt the production line.

Formatting the table and graph

Problems [delay in hours]	Occurrences	Total (h)	%	Cumulative %
Machine set-up [7]	56	392	37,95	37,95
Recalibration [3]	87	265	25,27	63,21
Bad configuration [4]	23	92	8,91	72,12
Machine oil leak [7]	12	84	8,13	80,25
Stock shortage [12]	5	60	5,81	86,06
Order changes [4]	15	60	5,81	91,87
Compressor failure [7]	4	28	2,71	94,58
Employee strike [24]	1	24	2,32	96,90
Power cut [1]	22	22	2,13	99,03
General breakdown [2]	5	10	0,97	100,00
Total	230	1033	100,00	

Pareto's Principle © 50MINUTES.com

- The first column shows the problems identified in the factory. The data in brackets is the number of hours of inactivity caused by each problem.
- In the second column, the number of occurrences is listed. In total, there are 230.
- The third column shows, in descending order, the results of multiplying the number of occurrences by the number of hours each stoppage causes. This gives the total number of hours of inactivity caused by each problem. This data will be used to plot the bars on the Pareto chart.
- The fourth column details the percentage of the total of lost working hours and the last column shows the cumulative percentages.

The graph below shows the data presented visually: the blue line (right axis) shows the cumulative percentage and the red bars are the number of hours of inactivity (left axis) caused by each problem.

Graph of the production line of the example industry

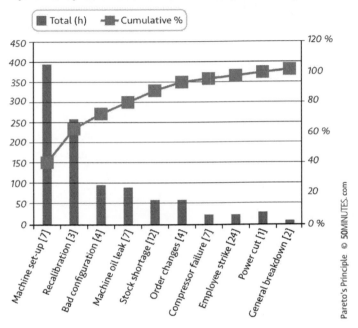

Identifying the important factors

Pareto's principle works particularly well in this case because a minority of factors cause the majority of problems. Specifically, almost 30% of the factors cause 72% of delays in the production line. Notice that there are two other ratios close to 80/20:

- When considering the two biggest causes (20%), the percentage of delays is 63%;
- When considering the four biggest problems (40%), the percentage of delays is 80%.

Which is the best ratio? This question is difficult to answer. However, it's clear that the overall ratio of 30% of factors causing 72% of delays is closest to Pareto's principle.

Unfortunately, this does not solve all problems:
- Firstly, we are left with many problematic factors to adjust, but choosing to focus on the first ratio (two main issues) would focus on a minority of causes causing the maximum number of consequences, which is precisely the objective of Pareto's principle;
- Secondly, if the plant manager wants to fix as many problems as possible, he has every reason to focus on the third ratio, correcting 40% of causes that cause 80% of delays in the production line.

CONCLUSION

In our example, we observed a production line affected by significant and recurring delays. This example, despite being fictional, is readily adaptable to all areas of a company (production, machinery, employees, customers, etc.). By identifying the most important problems, a company can find solutions to minimize its efforts and maximize results.

With Pareto's principle, and the ABC model alongside, companies can think differently and focus on the most important problems while keeping control of their core business. Since we assume that 'time is money', we can easily imagine that every entrepreneur and every person involved in a company can optimize existing processes to remain competitive. The same applies to some individuals to whom Pareto's principle is applicable.

SUMMARY

- Pareto's principle is a universal tool which shows that 20% of causes contribute to 80% of the effects. By identifying these causes, an organization can easily control the most important effects.
- There are many applications of this principle. They concern not only companies targeting productivity or customer relationships, but also many areas of daily life, such as managing a household.
- A concrete application of Pareto's principle is the management of company customers. In a traditional business, 20% of customers usually generate 80% of sales. By identifying these customers, the company can focus on them to improve profitability.
- The ABC model is related to Pareto's principle. It enhances it by taking into account the intermediate categories, which also generate effects. These intermediate categories are less important, but still worth considering.
- The Long Tail theory is also a complementary concept to Pareto's principle, mainly concerning online sales. The 80/20 ratio is checked and a company that can reduce its costs, particularly with the internet, can afford not to focus only on the most important 20%, but on all of its merchandise, even the products that sell less.
- Finally, Pareto's law can easily be put into practice with tables and graphs. These provide a comprehensive view of the problem and identify the effects. The company, organization or simple household can then focus on taking action to improve efficiency and profitability.

FURTHER READING

SOURCES

- Anderson (Chris), *La Longue Traîne. La nouvelle économie est là !*, London, Pearson, 2009.
- Cotter (John J.), *The 20 % Solution*, Hoboken, John Wiley & Sons, 1995.
- Coyne (Shawn), 'The Pareto Principle Meets the Long Tail', in *Steven Pressfield Online*, accessed 22nd May 2014. http://www.stevenpressfield.com/2012/11/the-pareto-principle-meets-the-long-tail/
- Dufour (Laurent), 'Efficacité du dirigeant : qu'est-ce que la loi de Pareto?', in *Le Blog du Dirigeant*, accessed 22nd May 2014. http://leblogdudirigeant.com/efficacite-du-dirigeant-quest-ce-que-la-loi-de-pareto/
- Juran (Joseph M.), *Quality Control Handbook*, New-York, McGraw-Hill, 1951.
- Koch (Richard), *The 80/20 Principle*, Londres, Nicholas Brealey Publishing, 1998.
- 'Les techniques et stratégies de prospection', in *Le site des profs de vente et de commerce*, accessed 22nd May 2014. http://www.les-coursdevente.fr/bacvente/Prospection/Des%20outils%20de%20segmentation%20des%20clients-prospects,%20Pareto,%20ABC,%20RFM.pdf
- Montanaro (Lisa), 'The Power of the Pareto Principle (aka the 80/20 Rule)', in *Lisa Montanaro. Purpose. Passion. Productivity*, accessed 22nd May 2014. http://www.lisamontanaro.com/2012/03/16/the-power-of-the-pareto-principle-aka-the-8020-rule/

- Reh (John F.), 'Pareto Principle – The 80-20 Rule', in *Management about*, accessed 22nd May 2014. http://management.about.com/cs/generalmanagement/a/Pareto081202.htm
- 'Understanding the Pareto Principle (The 80/20 Rule)', in *Better Explained*, accessed 22nd May 2014. http://betterexplained.com/articles/understanding-the-pareto-principle-the-8020-rule/
- Villemin (Gérard), 'Loi de Pareto', in *Nombres – Curiosités, théories et usages*, accessed 22nd May 2014. http://villemin.gerard.free.fr/aSocial/Pareto.htm

COMPLIMENTARY SOURCES

- Marshall (Perry), *80/20 Sales and Marketing*, Irvine, Entrepreneur Press, 2013.
- Savara (Sid), 'The Problem with the Pareto Principle', in *Personal Development Training with Sid Savara*, accessed 22nd May 2014. http://sidsavara.com/personal-productivity/the-problem-with-the-pareto-principle

www.50minutes.com

Publisher: Lemaitre Publishing
Rue Lemaitre 6 | BE-5000 Namur
info@lemaitre-editions.com

ISBN ebook: 978-2-8062-6586-9
Paper ISBN: 978-2-8062-6935-5
Cover photo: © Lisiane Detaille

Digital conception: **Primento**,
the digital partner of publishers.